Physics Experiments

Grades K–2

By
Cherie Winner

Illustrations by
Gary Mohrman

Published by Instructional Fair
an imprint of
Frank Schaffer Publications®

W9-BGU-552

Instructional Fair

Author: Cherie Winner

Frank Schaffer Publications®

Instructional Fair is an imprint of Frank Schaffer Publications.

Send all inquiries to:
Frank Schaffer Publications
8720 Orion Place
Columbus, OH 43240-2111

Hands-On Physics Experiments—Grades K–2

ISBN: 0-7424-2748-X

2 3 4 5 6 7 8 9 10 MAZ 10 09 08 07 06

Hands-On Table of Contents

Published by Instructional Fair. Copyright protected.

0-7424-2748-X *Hands-On Physics Experiments*

This book is designed to help your students build on their natural curiosity about the world around them. They will learn how to use the tools and methods of science to look for answers to their questions. The investigations described here support the new National Science Education Standards in their emphasis on science as a *process of inquiry*, rather than a recitation of facts.

Each activity includes an instruction page that is followed by a student reproducible page. Instruction pages begin with a question or guiding statement. This is followed by a materials list, step-by-step directions, suggestions for discussion, and helpful tips. The student pages feature a variety of activities that can be customized to the ability level of your students.

This book is based on the National Science Education Standards for Physical Science. The first section, Properties of Objects and Materials, covers what things are made of and what they are like. The second section, Position and Motion of Objects, focuses on where things are and how they move. The final section, Light, Heat, Electricity, and Magnetism, investigates what we generally think of as energy. Feel free to mix activities from different sections. While each experiment stands on its own, you may find that an activity in one section fits well with an activity in another.

At the end of each section, you will find a page of suggestions for further inquiry. Many of these link the Physical Science activities with other portions of the NSE Standards such as Science and Technology, Earth and Space Science, History and Nature of Science, and Science in Personal and Social Perspectives. They all provide additional opportunities for you and your students to explore the fascinating world of physics.

4

In this section, students will gain a deeper understanding of objects and materials they encounter in their daily life. They will explore qualities they can describe with words such as *shape, color,* and *ability to float.* They will also begin to examine qualities they can express with numbers such as *size, weight,* and *temperature.* They will gain skill in manipulating objects and in using measuring devices such as *rulers, balances,* and *thermometers.*

Your students will discover that many objects are made of two or more different materials such as *wood, paper,* and *metal,* and that the qualities of an object as a whole depend on the qualities of the materials that make up the object.

Finally, your students will delve into the differences between *liquids, solids,* and *gases.* They will find that some materials can exist in any of those three states, and can be changed from one state to another by heating or cooling. Students will use one of the most common and most important materials on Earth—water—to explore the processes of *evaporation, condensation, freezing,* and *thawing.*

"Objects have many observable properties. Those properties can be measured using tools, such as rulers, balances, and thermometers. Objects are made of one or more materials. Objects can be described by the properties of the materials from which they are made, and those properties can be used to separate or sort a group of objects or materials. Materials can exist in different states—solid, liquid, or gas. Some common materials, such as water, can be changed from one state to another by heating or cooling."

National Science Education Standards

0-7424-2748-X *Hands-On Physics Experiments*

Experiment 1 Different or the Same?

Students compare several properties of common objects.
Through the observation of common objects, children reflect on the similarities
and differences of the objects.

What You Need:

- An assortment of objects, each composed of one substance. Examples include a toothpick, wooden block, stick, string, metal pie plate, plastic cup, marble, note paper, paper plate, magazine, CD case, wire clothes hanger, towel, sock, pottery mug, rock, mirror.

- Activity sheet on page 7 for each student

What to Do:

1. Give your students time to handle all the objects.

2. Have each student (or team of students) choose one object to draw or write about on their data page. They will describe their object's color, shape, what material it is made of, and whether it occurs naturally or was made by humans.

3. Ask students to look for other objects that are like their chosen object in some way—same color, same material, etc. If they cannot find one in your collection, they can look around the room for an object that is similar.

Let's Talk About It:

Objects have many properties (or characteristics) we can observe. These properties can be used to sort objects into groups of similar things. Objects that differ in every other way might share a color or shape.

Teacher Tips:

Younger children might find it hard to distinguish between an object and its properties. Be certain they see that the same object can belong to different groups, depending on what properties are being used as the basis for sorting the objects.

0-7424-2748-X *Hands-On Physics Experiments*

Properties of Objects and Materials

Name _____

Date _____

Different or the Same?

Draw your object:

It is made of _____.

Another object made of the same material is _____.

Its color is _____.

Another object with the same color is _____.

Its shape is _____.

Another object with the same shape is _____.

It was   made by people   found in nature.   (circle one)

Another object with this quality is _____.

Experiment 2 Mix and Match

Students sort objects made of two or more materials.
Objects can be made of more than one material.

What You Need:

- Common classroom objects
- Activity sheet on page 9 for each student

What to Do:

1. Use a wooden pencil to demonstrate an object made of more than one material. In this case, graphite (a mineral), wood, the metal collar at the top, and the eraser.

2. Have each student team search the room for two objects that are made of more than one material. Each of their objects should include different combinations of materials.

3. After the students record their finds, share the results.

Let's Talk About It:

Students see some of the ways different materials can be combined to form everyday objects. Which combinations are most common in your student objects? Which combinations are the most unusual?

Teacher Tips:

Guide your students to look for objects made of just two or three different materials that are easy to identify. Anything more complex can bog them down.

0-7424-2748-X *Hands-On Physics Experiments*

Name ______________________________

Date ________________

Mix and Match

What objects did you find?

What are they made of?

Object #1

____

____

____

____

____

Object #2

____

____

____

____

____

Experiment 3 Sink or Swim

What kinds of materials float, and what kinds sink?
Objects and materials have observable properties.

What You Need:

- An assortment of small objects, each made of a single material. Examples are wooden toothpicks or spools, coins, metal paper clips, plastic paper clips, marbles, sticks, rocks, and chalk.

- A bowl or small pail for each team of students

- Source of water (tap, pitcher, or bucket)

- Towels for drying hands and tabletop

- Activity sheet on page 11 for each student

What to Do:

1. Have each group choose three items to test. Record the material of each in the space provided.
2. Place all the items in the bottom of the team's bowl. Gently pour water into the bowl.
3. Observe which objects float and which ones remain on the bottom of the bowl.

Let's Talk About It:

Students find that some materials float while others do not, and some do sometimes but not all the time. This area is fertile ground for further experiments.

Teacher Tips:

You might want to handle the water-pouring duties, to minimize spills.

Name _____

Date _____

Sink or Swim

What objects did you test?	What is each object made of?	Check whether it sinks or floats.	
		sinks ☐	floats ☐
		sinks ☐	floats ☐
		sinks ☐	floats ☐

0-7424-2748-X *Hands-On Physics Experiments*

Experiment 4 — Going Bowl-ing

Students learn that objects with the same function can be made of different materials. Objects can be described by the properties of the materials from which they are made.

What You Need:

- Several bowls made of different materials, such as paper, plastic, metal, wood, and ceramic

- Assortment of objects made of the same materials as your bowls. Examples are toothpicks or wooden blocks, notebook paper, metal paper clips or food cans, plastic bottles or bottle caps, and ceramic plates or figurines

- Activity sheet on page 13 for each student

What to Do:

1. Invite students to handle the bowls and compare their shapes and relative weights.
2. Ask: *Which would make the best soup bowl? Why? Which would be better to take on a camping trip? Why?*
3. Have your students sort the other objects, placing each object into the bowl made of the same material. Students may clip and fold the labels on the opposite page to place by their bowls.

Let's Talk About It:

A bowl can be made of any one of several kinds of materials. Discuss the advantages and disadvantages of each.

Going Bowl-ing

Which bowl is biggest around?_____

Which bowl is deepest?_____

Which bowl is heaviest?_____

These things are made of paper.	These things are made of wood.
These things are made of plastic.	These things are made of metal.
These things are made of ceramic.	These things are made of _____.

0-7424-2748-X *Hands-On Physics Experiments*

Experiment 5 Shaping Up

How does an object's shape relate to how we use it?
Objects have observable properties.

What You Need:

- Several bowls of any material (You can use the bowls from the previous activity.)

- Several plates and cups of any material

- Activity sheet on page 15 for each student

What to Do:

1. Give your students time to handle the objects and become familiar with them.

2. Show your students that, seen from above, the objects all have a similar shape (round). From the side, they have different shapes. Have students draw the objects from both views.

3. Discuss the uses of the items and how their different shapes suit them for different functions.
   Ask: *If you could have only one of these to eat and drink from, which would you choose? Why?*

Let's Talk About It:

The shape of an object helps determine its function. Likewise, the function of an object helps determine its shape. *What other functions could these shapes (bowl, plate, cup) fulfill?*

Teacher Tips:

This activity works best if all the objects appear round when viewed from above. The cups may have a handle, but square plates and oval bowls might be confusing.

0-7424-2748-X *Hands-On Physics Experiments*

Name _____

Date _____

Shaping Up

What do the objects look like from above?

plate   bowl   cup

What do the objects look like from the side?

plate   bowl   cup

Experiment 6 Weighing In

Students compare the weights of two fruits.
Properties can be measured with tools.

What You Need:

- A balance or scale with an assortment of standard weights

- A variety of fruits of comparable size, such as an apple, orange, and pear; or berries, cherries, and grapes

- Activity sheet on page 17 for each student

What to Do:

1. Have your students lift two different fruits and guess which is heavier.

2. Ask them: *How can we use the balance to find out which fruit is heavier?* Show them how to zero the balance before weighing their fruits and how to read the weight of an object on the balance.

3. Have students weigh each of their fruits individually and record the results.

4. After doing step #3 above, use a two-pan balance to weigh the fruits to compare their weights. Place one fruit on one pan and the other fruit on the other pan. *Which is heavier? Using the standard weights, how much must be added to make the pans balance? To which side do you add the additional weights?*

Let's Talk About It:

While learning to use a balance, students also learn that they can weigh objects individually and then compare the results. They can also weigh two objects against each other for a direct comparison.

0-7424-2748-X *Hands-On Physics Experiments*

Name _____

Date _____

Weighing In

Draw your two fruits.

Draw a circle around the fruit that feels heavier to you.

 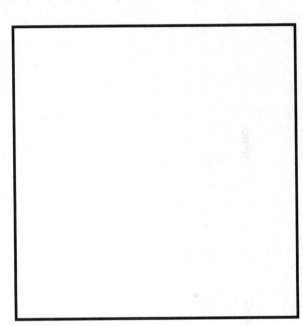

How much do the fruits weigh?

Fruit #1 _____   Fruit #2 _____

The _____ weighs _____ more than

the _____.

Experiment 7 — The Measure of Me

Students make "rulers" based on their own hands.
Properties can be measured using tools.

What You Need:

- Cardboard or stiff paper cut into strips 9–12 inches long and 2–3 inches wide

- Large classroom objects such as chairs and desks

- Activity sheet on page 19 for each student

What to Do:

1. Have each student spread a hand wide open along the line on their activity page and mark the widest span.

2. Show students how to lay a cardboard strip on the plain paper and mark their spread hand on the cardboard strip. Their spread-hand distance is their personal unit of measure. They can trim the ends of the strip, but they should leave the strip a bit longer than their spread-hand for ease of handling.

3. Let students measure the height, width, and length of a classroom object with their personal rulers. Be certain that each object is measured by at least two students.

4. Compare measurements of the same object made by different students.

Let's Talk About It:

The first units of measurement were probably based on a personal measurement such as a spread-hand. *What's good and what's not so good about using a personal unit of measure such as this?*

Teacher Tips:

Few objects will fit into a complete number of "hands." Show students that they can fold their rulers in half to measure half-units. Beyond that, they will have to round up or round down to the next nearest whole-unit measurement.

The Measure of Me

On this line, mark how long your hand measure is:

_____

Draw the object you measured:

How big is it?

_____ hands tall

_____ hands wide

_____ hands long

Did any other students measure the same object with their hand rulers?

What sizes did they get? _____

Experiment 8 Setting Standards

Students measure classroom objects with standard rulers.
Objects can be measured with standard units.

What You Need:

- 12-inch rulers

- An assortment of classroom objects. Include those used in the previous activity and some smaller items such as books and pencil boxes.

- Activity sheet on page 21 for each student

What to Do:

1. Show your students how to read the markings on the rulers. Explain that the ruler's total length is one foot, each foot contains 12 inches, and each inch is the same length.

2. Have students measure the height, width, and length of an object. Be certain that some students measure the same objects used in the previous exercise and some measure objects that are shorter than the rulers.

3. After the students record their measurements, share the results.

Let's Talk About It:

Using standard units of measure allows easier comparison than in the previous activity when every student used a different unit of measurement. *In this activity, was it easier to measure small objects or large ones?* Invite students to share ideas for making measuring easier and more accurate.

Teacher Tips:

The words *height*, *width*, and *length* can be confusing because they depend on how an object is oriented. For example, a book lying on a table is long and wide, but very short in height; the same book placed upright on a shelf is taller but not as wide.

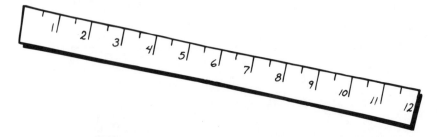

Name _____

Date _____

Setting Standards

Draw the object you measured:

How big is it?

_____ tall

_____ wide

_____ long

Did any other students measure the same object with their standard rulers?

What sizes did they get? _____

0-7424-2748-X *Hands-On Physics Experiments*

Experiment 9 — Material World

Students observe the properties of solids and liquids.
Materials in different states have different properties.

What You Need:

- Small block or stick of wood

- Modeling clay

- Objects made of clear, hard plastic, such as cups or rulers

- Water

- Soy sauce

- Hand lotion

- Small bowls or saucers for the liquids

- Activity sheet on page 23 for each student

What to Do:

1. Give each team a piece of wood, some clay, a plastic item, and a small amount of the three liquids. Help them to explore whether each material can change its shape easily (that is, bend or flow); whether the material holds its shape by itself; and whether the students can see through it. Define the terms *transparent* and *opaque*.

2. Help students record their results on their data page. Ask: *In what ways are solids and liquids different?*

Let's Talk About It:

Observing properties such as shape and transparency helps us recognize that liquids may be like solids in some ways and different from solids in other ways.

Teacher Tips:

Note that the two questions about shape are not mutually exclusive. For example, the clay will bend easily, but it also holds whatever shape you make it.

Name _____

Date _____

Material World

Things you tested		It holds its shape	It changes shape easily	You can see through it	You can't see through it
Solids	wood				
	clay				
	plastic				
Liquids	water				
	soy sauce				
	hand lotion				

Experiment 10 Strong Air

Students show that air can be stronger than water.

Gases have observable properties.

What You Need:

- Clear cups or glasses
- Bowl that is deeper than the cups are tall
- Water
- Food coloring
- Activity sheet on page 25 for each student

What to Do:

1. Fill the bowl with water. Add several drops of food coloring and stir to spread it all through the water.
2. Have your students each turn a cup upside down and gently press it straight down into the water. Be careful not to tilt the cup. Ask: *What do you see inside the cup?*
3. Slowly tilt the cup until a few bubbles of air escape. Ask: *Now what do you see inside the cup?*

Let's Talk About It:

This experiment shows that air is a substance that occupies space and can exert force on another substance (water). Air under the inverted cup pushes down on the water and keeps it from coming into the cup. When some air leaves via the bubbles, the space it took up inside the cup can be filled by water.

0-7424-2748-X *Hands-On Physics Experiments*

Name _____

Date _____

Strong Air

What did you see inside the cup?

After you tilted the cup, what did you see inside it?

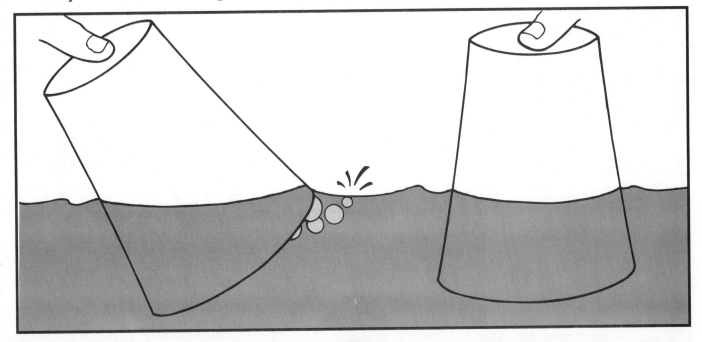

0-7424-2748-X *Hands-On Physics Experiments*

Experiment 11 Disappearing Water

Students make water "disappear."
Water can be changed from one state to another by heating or cooling.

What You Need:

- Identical bowls or containers for each group. (Oleo tubs work well.)

- Water

- Measuring cup

- Waterproof marking pen

- Two thermometers

- Two places to place the water samples: one warm, such as a spot under a desk lamp; and one cool, such as a shelf in a shaded corner

- Activity sheet on page 27 for each student

What to Do:

1. Measure and record the temperature at each of your two sites.
2. Set containers at each site. Measure ¼ cup of water into each container. Mark the starting water level on each container along with the team's name or number.
3. After three days, mark the water level in each container again.

Let's Talk About It:

The water evaporated more quickly from the warm site because higher temperature aids in the transition from liquid (water) to gas (water vapor).

Teacher Tips:

Younger students may have trouble with the concept of water becoming a gas. The experiment "Out of Thin Air" on page 30 will help them see that water vapor is in the air all around us.

26

Name _____

Date _____

Disappearing Water

Draw your container and draw arrows to show how high the water reached.

At the start of the experiment, the water came up to here.

At the end of the experiment, the water came up to here.

Your water sample was in the   **warm**   **cool**   spot. (circle one)

The temperature there was _____.

Experiment 12 The Big Freeze

How does water change when it freezes?
Water expands when it changes from liquid to solid.

What You Need:

- Small plastic containers, such as pill bottles or glasses

- Bowls

- Water

- Waterproof marker

- Freezer

- Activity sheet on page 29 for each student

What to Do:

1. Use a marker to write each team's name or number on its container. Fill each container about half-full of water. Draw a line on the container to show the level of the water.

2. Place the containers in a freezer. Be careful not to spill or splash any of the water.

3. After the water has frozen solid (later that day or the next day), mark the location of the top of the ice.

4. Leave the frozen samples out at room temperature until they thaw completely. Check the water level again.

Let's Talk About It:

When water freezes, its crystalline structure makes it expand. When the ice melts, the water returns to its original level. This is why ice and frost can crack rocks and pavement.

Teacher Tips:

Not all liquids expand when they freeze. This is a peculiar trait of water/ice.

Name _____

Date _____

The Big Freeze

Draw a line to show where the top of the water was at the start of the experiment.

Draw a line to show where the top of the ice was.

Draw a line to show where the top of the water was at the end of the experiment.

0-7424-2748-X *Hands-On Physics Experiments*

Experiment 13 Out of Thin Air

Does air really contain water?
Water can be changed from one state to another by heating or cooling.

What You Need:

- Vertical plastic containers, such as pill bottles or plastic glasses
- Water
- Waterproof marker
- Freezer
- Activity sheet on page 31 for each student

What to Do:

1. Mark each team's name or number on its container. Fill each container about half-full of water. Mark the water level on the containers.
2. Place containers in the freezer. Be careful not to spill or splash any of the water.
3. After the water has frozen solid (later that day or the next day), set them out at room temperature. After 15 to 30 minutes, check the containers. *Is the ice melting? What do you see on the outside of the containers?* Ask: *Did the water droplets there come from inside the container? How do you know?*

Let's Talk About It:

Water droplets form on the outside of the containers as the ice melts. They do not come from the water inside the containers, because the original water level does not go down. They form when water vapor in the air is cooled so much by contact with the cold container that it changes from a gas to a liquid. This change is called *condensation*. Ask: *Where else do we see condensation?*

Teacher Tips:

Air is a mixture of many gases, including oxygen, nitrogen, and hydrogen, in addition to water vapor.

Out of Thin Air

What your container looked like when you took it out of the freezer:

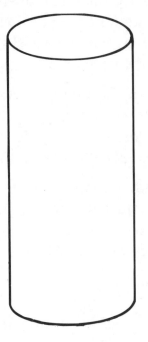

What your container looked like after the ice had melted:

Encourage students to compare common objects in their classrooms and homes. Have them speculate about why objects were made of certain materials. *Would another material have been better in some ways? Worse in some ways?* Consider factors such as the materials' strength, flexibility, softness, ability to float, visual appeal, and cost to obtain or manufacture.

Have students look for objects made of two or more materials. *Why were these different materials used, rather than making the object out of just one kind of material? Does each material contribute some necessary quality to the object? Why is a material such as plastic sometimes made to look like wood?*

A few months after students make a measuring device based on their own hand, have them make a new one and compare it with the original. *Is the new one a different size? By how much?* Have the students use their new "ruler" to re-measure an item they measured before.

After a rain, have students track what happens to puddles near their classroom. You could also make artificial puddles. *Why did the puddles form where they did? How deep is the water in each puddle? Do some puddles dry up faster than others? Why?* Consider such factors as depth, drainage, and exposure to sunshine and wind.

If you have an aquarium in the classroom, have the students keep track of how quickly the water level drops, and how often they must add water to the tank.

In this section, your students will describe the position of an object in relation to things around it. They will set an object into motion and explore how fast and how far it moves in response to being pushed, pulled, and rolled down ramps of different heights. As the object moves, students will figure out how to describe and measure its movement. Their investigations will introduce them to levers and to important concepts such as gravity, force, and friction.

Finally, your students will experiment with how sound is made. They are already very good at making noise. They will now look more closely at this natural event. They will find that all sounds, including their own voices, result from vibrations. That is why the National Science Education Standards include Sound in the section on objects in motion. Some teachers prefer to teach Sound in their discussions of Energy (section 3). Either way, questions about how sound is created and transmitted make a good link between a study unit on motion and one on energy.

"The position of an object can be described by locating it relative to another object or the background. An object's motion can be described by tracing and measuring its position over time. The position and motion of an object can be changed by pushing or pulling. The size of the change is related to the strength of the push or pull. Sound is produced by vibrating objects. The pitch of the sound can be varied by changing the rate of vibration."

National Science Education Standards

Experiment 14 Where Is It?

Students describe the location of a classroom object.
The position of an object can be described by locating it relative to other objects and the background.

What You Need:

- Student teams positioned at different places in the room

- Activity sheet on page 35 for each student

What to Do:

1. Position each student team in a different part of the room. Have each team quietly select an object in the room. It can be any size, but must be stationary and in plain sight. Students should not draw or name their object on their maps. It must be kept a secret!

2. From their viewpoint in the room, ask each group to identify other objects *in front of, behind, to the left,* and *to the right of* their secret object. They then draw or name these "signpost" objects on their maps.

3. When the maps are done, have teams trade maps and positions. Using another team's map, can they figure out the other team's secret object?

Let's Talk About It:

We can describe where an object is by using phrases like "in front of" and "to the left of." However, such descriptions depend on where we are relative to the object we're describing.

Name _____

Date _____

Where Is It?

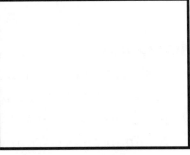

This is behind our
secret object.

This is to the left of
our secret object.

This is our
secret object.

This is to the right of
our secret object.

This is in front of
our secret object.

You are HERE, looking this way.

0-7424-2748-X *Hands-On Physics Experiments*

Experiment 15 Move It

Students change the position of an object.
Objects can be moved by pulling or pushing.

What You Need:

- An assortment of common objects. Examples are books, crayons, chairs, drinking glasses, pencil boxes, zippers, string, tennis balls, and towels.

- Activity sheet on page 37 for each student

What to Do:

1. Ask your students: *What is the difference between pushing and pulling?*
2. Invite your students to try pushing and pulling several common objects from your collection.

Let's Talk About It:

Students begin to recognize that pulling brings an object closer to the force making it move, while pushing sends an object away from the force making it move.

Teacher Tips:

Stick with clear, simple movements. Many movements such as writing involve intricate combinations of pushing and pulling. These movements may be too complex for younger students to analyze.

Name _____

Date _____

Move It

Draw an arrow to show which way the wagon will go if the boy pushes it.

Draw an arrow to show which way the wagon will go if the boy pulls it.

0-7424-2748-X *Hands-On Physics Experiments*

Experiment 16 Launch Pad

What controls how far an object will go?

The size of an object's change in position is related to the strength of the force acting on it.

What You Need:

- Plastic 12-inch rulers
- Plastic bottle caps
- Modeling clay
- Activity sheet on page 39 for each student

What to Do:

1. Stick a bit of clay on one end of the ruler so it makes a low rim. Set the ruler on a desk or table so that the 6-inch mark lines up with the edge of the table, and the end of the ruler with the clay rim extends past the table's edge. Hold the ruler in place by pressing down on it as close to the table edge as you can.

2. Set a bottle cap on the free end of the ruler. The clay rim will keep it from falling off.

3. Gently pull the free end of the ruler down just a bit—about a half inch. Let it go. *What happens to the bottle cap? How far up does it go?*

4. Try launching the bottle cap again, this time pulling the end of the ruler down about an inch before releasing it. Note how far the bottle cap goes. Launch again, pulling the end of the ruler down 2–3 inches.

Let's Talk About It:

The more the ruler is bent, the harder it pushes on the bottle cap and the higher the cap goes. Students might be able to feel the ruler pushing back more as they pull it down farther. When they let go, that force is transmitted to the bottle cap.

Name _____

Date _____

Launch Pad

Show how high the bottle cap flew.

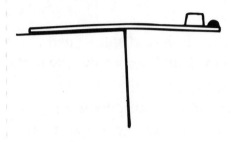

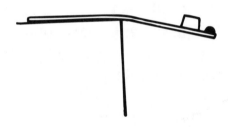

0-7424-2748-X *Hands-On Physics Experiments*

Experiment 17 Rebound

Students follow a ball as it strikes and bounces off a wall.
An object's motion can be described by tracing the change in its position over time.

What You Need:

- Tennis balls

- Wall or other vertical surface with a few feet of clear space in front of it

- Yarn or string

- Activity sheet on page 41 for each student

What to Do:

1. Give each student team a tennis ball and some yarn. Have students practice rolling the ball smoothly toward the wall from about two feet away.

2. Have students use the yarn to make a line from the ball to the wall. Using that line as a guide, have them roll the ball toward the wall and notice where it goes after it bounces off. Have them lay down another piece of yarn along the path of the rebound. Help students draw a line on their activity page to show the path their ball took.

3. Invite students to try rolling the ball so it strikes the wall at different angles. Help them draw lines to show the rebound paths.

Let's Talk About It:

A ball will bounce off at the same angle at which it struck the wall. A ball hitting the wall straight on will bounce straight back toward the starting point; a ball hitting at a slight angle will rebound at a slight angle; and a ball hitting at a wide angle will rebound at an equally wide angle.

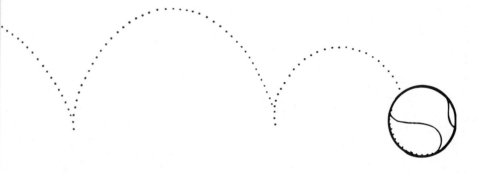

Name _____

Date _____

Rebound

Draw lines to show where the ball went after it hit the wall.

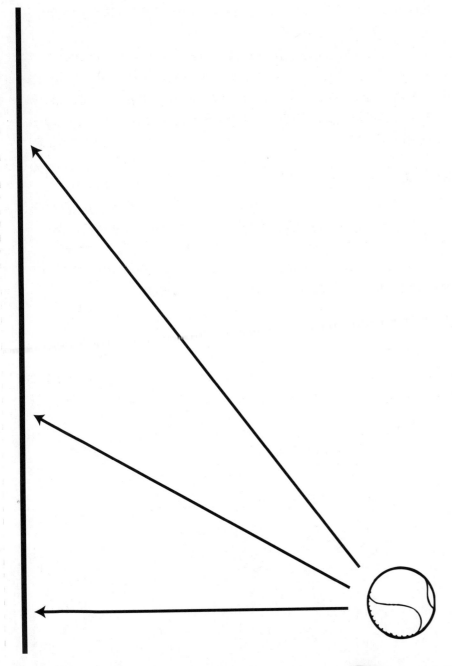

0-7424-2748-X *Hands-On Physics Experiments*

Experiment 18 Pop the Top

Students learn that levers can help them move heavy loads.
A lever magnifies the force applied to an object.

What You Need:

- Can of cocoa with lid (the can may be empty)

- Screwdriver

- Activity sheet on page 43 for each student

What to Do:

1. With the lid firmly in place on the cocoa can, have several students try to remove it. (Some might succeed, but only with difficulty.)

2. Ask your students: *How could we use a screwdriver to help remove the lid?* Guide them in using the screwdriver as a lever with the edge of the can as the fulcrum. Let all students try it to see how easy it is to remove the lid.

Let's Talk About It:

Draw a lever and fulcrum on the board. Show the load (in this case, the lid) at one end of the lever and the force (a person pushing down) at the other end. Can the students think of any other examples of a lever? Candidates include paint can lids, a jack for lifting a car, and a seesaw.

0-7424-2748-X *Hands-On Physics Experiments*

Pop the Top

Draw arrows to show where you pushed down, and what moved up.

Where is the fulcrum?

Experiment 19 Easy Does It

Where is the best place to put the fulcrum and load?

Placing a load closer to the fulcrum of a lever makes it easier to lift.

What You Need:

- Spring-type clothespins, enough for each pair of students to have one

- Activity sheet on page 45 for each student

What to Do:

1. Have each pair of students set their clothespin on a desk and press on the free end to see that the clothespin is a lever. The spring is the fulcrum, the pincher end is where the load goes, and the free end is where they apply the force.

2. Ask your students: *Do you think one partner can hold the clothespin shut while the other presses on the lever?*

3. With the clothespin resting on a desk, have one member of each team press down on the load end while the other team member presses on the free end. *Does the clothespin open? How hard does the load person have to push to keep it closed?*

4. Now have the load student push down very close to the fulcrum. Again, let the other student press on the free end. *Does the clothespin open? What if the load person pushes as hard as possible?*

Let's Talk About It:

A load placed closer to the fulcrum is much easier to lift, so the clothespin will be hard to open when the load student pushes at the far end. However, it will open easily no matter how hard the load student pushes near the fulcrum.

0-7424-2748-X *Hands-On Physics Experiments*

Name _____

Date _____

Easy Does It

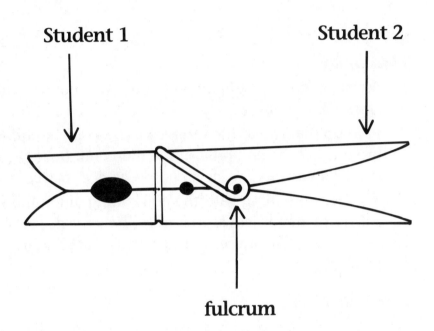

Student 1   Student 2

fulcrum

Did it open?

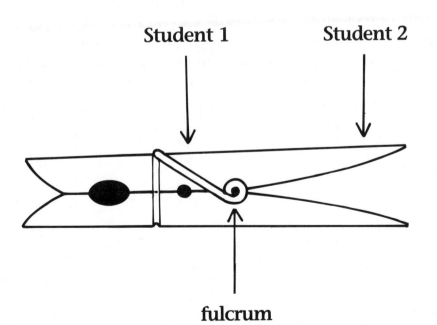

Student 1   Student 2

fulcrum

Did it open?

0-7424-2748-X *Hands-On Physics Experiments*

Experiment 20 Start/Stop

Students explore what makes things start and stop moving.
Objects move when a force pushes or pulls on them.

What You Need:

- Tennis balls

- Clipboards or other flat, smooth objects that can be used as ramps

- Yardsticks

- Variety of surfaces, such as smooth tile floor, carpeted floor, coarse sandpaper

- Activity sheet on page 47 for each student

What to Do:

1. Set the ball on a ramp lying flat on the floor. *Does the ball move?*

2. Prop up one end of the ramp so it is 3–4 inches off the ground. Set the ball on it at the high end. *Does the ball move?* Measure how far it goes. *Why does it stop?*

3. Try the same thing with the ball rolling onto different surfaces when it leaves the ramp. *How far does the ball go on each roll?* Be certain to start from the same height each time.

Let's Talk About It:

The ball does not move on a flat ramp because of inertia— the tendency of an object to stay put until a force acts on it. Tilting the ramp allows a force (gravity) to pull the ball downward. The ball eventually stops moving because it is on a level surface, so gravity cannot pull it any lower and because of friction from the surface. Rougher surfaces have more friction than smooth ones and stop the ball sooner.

0-7424-2748-X *Hands-On Physics Experiments*

Name _____

Date _____

Start/Stop

Did the ball move?

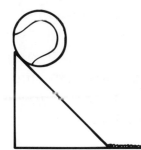

smooth floor

How far did the ball roll?_____ inches

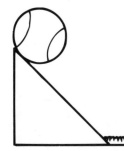

sandpaper

How far did the ball roll?_____ inches

carpet

How far did the ball roll?_____ inches

0-7424-2748-X *Hands-On Physics Experiments*

Experiment 21 Farther and Faster

What makes an object go farther or faster?
The speed and size of a movement is related to the strength of the forces acting on it.

What You Need:

- Several clipboards or other flat, smooth objects that can be used as ramps

- Books

- Tennis balls

- Clear floor space

- Yardsticks

- Activity sheet on page 49 for each student

What to Do:

1. Make ramps of different slopes by using different numbers of books to support the high end of each ramp. Record the height of the upper end of each ramp. Be certain that each ramp is the same length.

2. Hold a tennis ball at the top of each ramp, then let the balls go. Do not push them or otherwise help them along.

3. Watch how fast and how far each ball goes.

Let's Talk About It:

Balls rolling from steeper ramps go faster and farther because the steeper slope allows them to build up more speed.

Teacher Tips:

Older students can measure the height of each ramp and the distance traveled; younger children can use descriptive terms such as *lowest*, *highest*, and *farthest*.

0-7424-2748-X *Hands-On Physics Experiments*

Farther and Faster

Show how far the balls went.

_____

_____

_____

Experiment 22 Salt Shakers

How are sounds made?
Sound is produced by vibrations.

What You Need:

- Glass bowl or empty metal food can
- Plastic wrap
- Rubber band
- Salt
- 1-quart metal cooking pot
- Metal spoon
- Activity sheet on page 51 for each student

What to Do:

1. Stretch the plastic wrap over the bowl or the end of the metal can and attach with the rubber band. Sprinkle salt on the plastic wrap.
2. Holding the pot so its open side is toward the salt, bang on the bottom of the pot with the spoon. Watch what the salt does.
3. Experiment with banging the pot at different distances and directions away from the salt.

Let's Talk About It:

Banging on the pot makes it vibrate, which creates vibrations in the air nearby. Those vibrations are sound waves. When the vibrations hit the salt grains, the grains jump. The plastic wrap makes it easier to see the salt move. It is very sensitive to vibrations in the air, much like our eardrums. Salt sprinkled on a tabletop will not be as lively as salt on a thin plastic membrane.

Name _____

Date _____

Salt Shakers

Show what the salt did when you banged on the pot.

bang

0-7424-2748-X *Hands-On Physics Experiments*

Experiment 23 Musical Rulers

What makes sounds higher or lower?
The pitch of a sound depends on the length of the vibrating object.

What You Need:

- Plastic rulers

- Desks or tables with straight, flat edges

- Activity sheet on page 53 for each student

What to Do:

1. Place a ruler on a table so its 8-inch mark is at the edge of the table and 4 inches of the ruler extends past the table. Hold the ruler in place by pressing on it with one hand as close to the edge of the table as you can.

2. Strum the free end of the ruler. Notice the pitch of the sound it makes (high, low, or in-between).

3. Move the ruler so the 8½-inch mark lines up with the table edge. Hold it firmly in place and strum it again. *Does it sound different?* Then move the ruler the other direction, so the 9-inch mark lines up with the table edge. Strum. *What does it sound like now?*

4. Let your students explore how strumming different lengths of ruler creates sounds of different pitch.

Let's Talk About It:

A longer object creates slower vibrations and a lower pitch. A shorter object creates faster vibrations and a higher pitch. Students will hear a clear difference between the different ruler positions and will also see the ruler vibrating after it is strummed.

0-7424-2748-X *Hands-On Physics Experiments*

Name _____

Date _____

Musical Rulers

Circle the ruler that will make the lowest note when it vibrates.

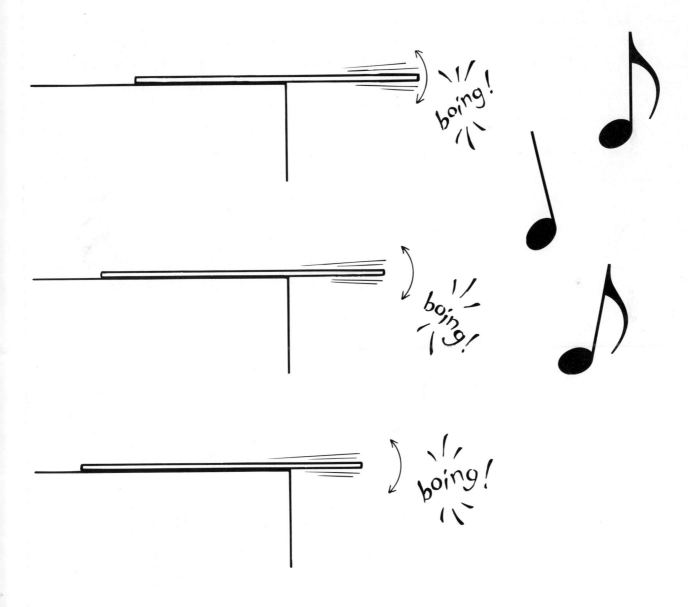

Experiment 24 Hummm

How do people make higher and lower notes?
The pitch of a sound depends on the length of the vibrating object.

What You Need:

- Students in a musical mood

- Activity sheet on page 55 for each student

What to Do:

1. Remind your students that the ruler experiment showed that longer objects create lower notes than shorter objects. Ask: *Do you think the human voice works the same way? What vibrates when people talk or sing?*

2. Have students hum softly.
    Do they feel vibrations in their throat, mouth, or head? Where do they make an effort when they change notes?

3. Show students how to place their fingertips gently on the front of their throat to feel the vibrations when they hum.
    Where are the vibrations when they hum a low note? Where are the vibrations when they hum a higher note?

4. Help students mark on their activity sheets where they felt the vibrations.

Let's Talk About It:

Our vocal cords are in the part of the throat called the *larynx*. We hum by passing air over the cords and making both the cords and the air vibrate. Lower notes come from a long column of air that reaches low in the throat; higher notes come from a short column of air near the top of the throat.

Hummm

Show where you feel vibrations.
when you hum a very high note.

Show where you feel vibrations
when you hum a middle note.

Show where you feel vibrations
when you hum a very low note.

0-7424-2748-X *Hands-On Physics Experiments*

A fun variation on the map-making activity is to secretly assign the same object to two teams describing it from different viewpoints. Then have them exchange places and try to identify the other team's object from the other team's map. Looking at the same object from different positions provides an early lesson in relativity.

Encourage your students to look for the forces that cause things to move. *Where do they see pushing and pulling at work in everyday life? Can they find cases where an object is both pushed and pulled? Is one action better than the other in some situations?*

The playground is a great place to explore the concepts introduced in this section. Swings can be pushed or pulled, seesaws show that levers can be fun, the smoothness of your clothing affects how fast you can slip down a slide, and games involving a ball provide opportunities to experiment with rebound angles.

If you have access to a musical instrument, let students watch closely as it is played. *Can they spot the part that vibrates to produce sound? What happens to the sound if they press on the vibrating part to restrict its movement? Can they tell how the instrument makes sounds of different pitch?*

All throughout this section, younger students can use descriptive terms such as *farther* and *faster*. Older students can be encouraged to measure specific distances, weights, and times.

In this section, your students will explore many forms of energy. They will watch a beam of light as it crosses a room, see what happens when it strikes solid objects, and puzzle over how it reflects off a mirror. They will learn several ways to produce heat, and how some objects transmit heat while others block it.

Your students will build a simple circuit to convert electricity into light energy. They will find that electrical currents require a complete loop or circuit in order to work, and they will build a switch that turns a current on and off.

Finally, they will have fun testing how magnets interact with each other and with other objects.

During their explorations in this section, students will develop skill in handling sources of heat, light, and electricity. Safety is a key concern here. Be certain that your students know that energy must always be handled with care. In particular, water and electricity are a very dangerous combination.

"Light travels in a straight line until it strikes an object. Light can be reflected by a mirror, refracted by a lens, or absorbed by the object. Heat can be produced in many ways, such as burning, rubbing, or mixing one substance with another. Heat can move from one object to another by conduction. Electricity in circuits can produce light, heat, sound, and magnetic effects. Magnets attract and repel each other and certain kinds of other materials."

National Science Education Standards

Experiment 25 High Beams

Students find that light does not bend.
Light travels in a straight line until it strikes an object.

What You Need:

- Flashlight

- Paper tube such as those in rolls of bathroom tissue or paper towels

- Tape

- Chalk dust or talcum powder

- Darkened room

- Activity sheet on page 59 for each student

What to Do:

1. Tape the paper tube to the lamp end of the flashlight so the tube helps direct the light into a narrow beam.

2. Darken the room. Holding the flashlight vertically, shine it toward the ceiling. Show your students that moving the flashlight moves the spot.

3. With the flashlight on, ask: *Can you see the beam of light? If you couldn't see the spot of light on the ceiling, would you be able to tell the light was on?*

4. Shake a little chalk dust or talcum powder into the air above the flashlight. *What do the students see now?*

Let's Talk About It:

The light travels straight from the flashlight to the ceiling, so we cannot see the beam from the side. When dust particles are struck by the beam, they light up and help us see where the beam is.

High Beams

Draw what you saw when the flashlight was turned on.

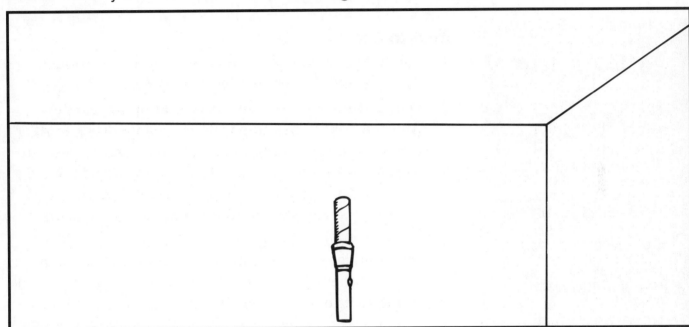

Draw what you saw when the flashlight was turned on and dust was sprinkled in the air above it.

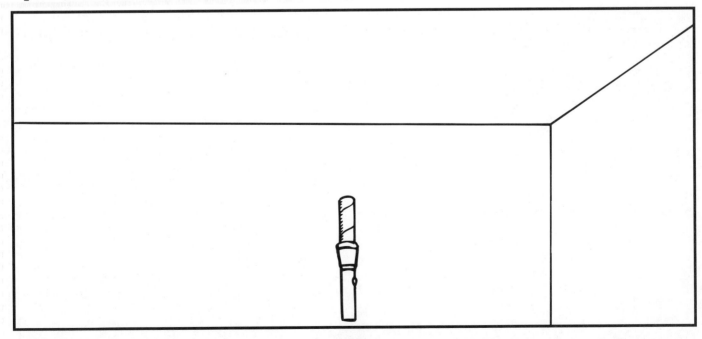

0-7424-2748-X *Hands-On Physics Experiments*

Experiment 26 Shadow Shapes

Students learn how to make shadows of different shapes.
Light travels in a straight line until it strikes an object.

What You Need:

- Pale wall or other vertical background

- Slide projector or desk lamp

- Two yardsticks or rulers

- Opaque objects such as scissors, spatula, spoon, comb, plant, pencil, book

- Darkened room

- Activity sheet on page 61 for each student

What to Do:

1. Remind your students that light travels in a straight line. Ask: *What happens when light strikes an object?*

2. Darken the room and turn on the lamp or projector. Aim the light at the pale wall. Hold a yardstick or ruler crosswise in the beam of light. Have a student measure its shadow on the wall. Rotate the yardstick so the light hits it at an angle. *What happens to its shadow?* Keep rotating the yardstick until it is parallel to the beam of light. *How big is its shadow now?*

4. Invite students to suggest other objects to experiment with. Let them explore how a shadow changes size and shape as its object is turned within the beam of light.

Let's Talk About It:

Light does not pass through opaque objects. The area directly behind the object will be unlit and form a shadow. Objects can often be recognized by their shadows, but it depends on how they are oriented with respect to the light.

Shadow Shapes

Draw lines to match the object with its shadow.

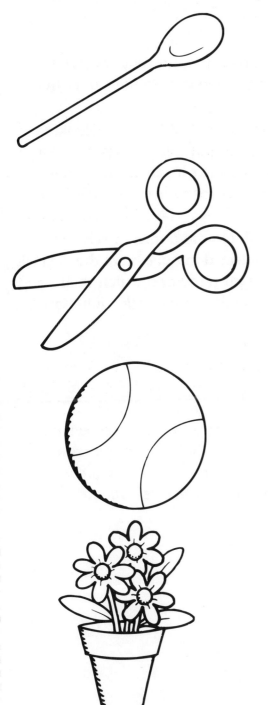

Experiment 27 The Same, Only Backwards

Students explore the properties of mirrors and reflections.
A mirror reflects light and creates an image in which left and right are reversed.

What You Need:

- An assortment of mirrors
- Washable markers
- Activity sheet on page 63 for each student

What to Do:

1. Have students use a marker to put a spot of color on their right cheeks. Group students into pairs and give each pair a mirror.

2. Have partners face each other as if they were looking into a mirror. Where is their partner's red spot? Have them touch their own red spot with their right hand. *When they do this, where is their partner's right hand— to the left, or to the right?*

3. Now have each student look into a mirror. Where is their red spot in their reflected image? Have them touch the red spot with their right hand and watch their reflected image. *Which hand of their reflection moves, the left or the right?*

Let's Talk About It:

Mirrors provide a reflection that is reversed left-to-right (but not, oddly enough, top-to-bottom). Students can also look in the mirror for other features that are on just one side. Examples include the part in their hair, a birthmark, or a missing tooth. *When they see the reflection of someone behind them, is that person behind their left shoulder or their right shoulder?*

Name _____

Date _____

The Same, Only Backwards

Show where the red spot is on your partner's face:

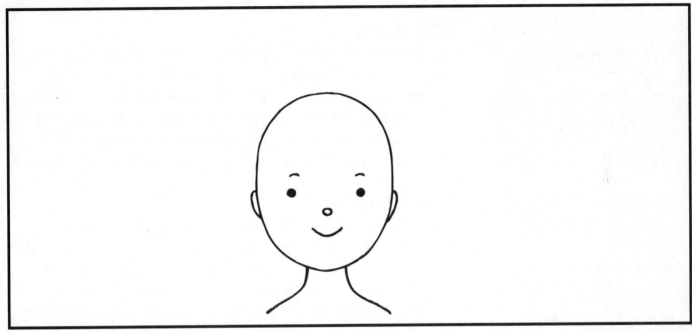

Show where the red spot is on the reflection of your own face:

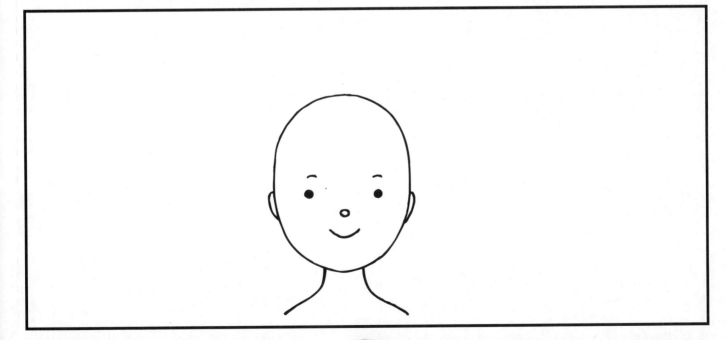

0-7424-2748-X *Hands-On Physics Experiments*

Experiment 28 Warming Up

Where does heat come from?

Heat can be produced in many ways, including friction, electricity, and light.

What You Need:

- Two electric heating pads, one turned on and one turned off

- Bowl of cool water

- Bowl of warm water

- Block of wood

- Sandpaper

- Sunny windowsill

- Shaded table

- Activity sheet on page 65 for each student

What to Do:

1. Set up the experimental items in a place where all students can handle them. Invite students to touch the heating pads, dip a finger into the water, touch the sunny spot and a shaded spot close by, and touch the block of wood before and after sanding it for several seconds.

2. *What do students notice about all the items they touch?*

Let's Talk About It:

In this activity, heat is made by sunlight, friction, and electricity. Other possible sources include fire and chemical reactions. *What made the water warm?* Explain that some water heaters heat with electricity and some use fire (by burning natural gas). If possible, visit the room that houses the school's water heater to find out how it works.

Teacher Tips:

You might have to refill the bowl with warm water during the experiment.

Warming Up

Which was warmer?

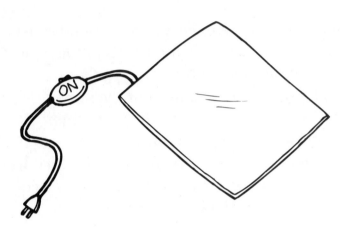

on

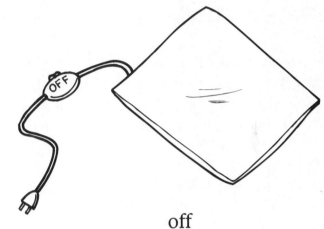

off

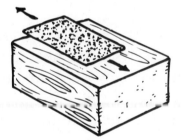

sanded

not sanded

sunny spot

shady spot

Experiment 29 · Heat Moves

What kinds of materials transfer heat, and what kinds don't?
Heat can move from one object to another by conduction.

What You Need:

- Assortment of cups and mugs made of various materials. Examples include plastic foam, plastic, metal, and pottery. They should all be roughly the same diameter.

- Hot water

- Measuring cup

- Thermometers, one per cup

- Clock or watch

- Activity sheet on page 67 for each student

What to Do:

1. Set the cups on a table where they will not be disturbed for fifteen minutes. Be certain that all parts of the table are at about the same temperature.

2. Assign each cup to a student team. Pour the same amount of hot water into each cup. Have students record the temperature of their sample.

3. Check the temperature again after five minutes. Feel the outside of the cup. *Is it warm? Cool? In-between?* Check the temperature again at fifteen minutes.

4. Compare results. Which cup kept the water warm the longest? The shortest?

Let's Talk About It:

Hot water in a metal cup will quickly lose its heat to the metal. Hot water in a foam cup will stay warm and the cup will stay cool. Materials that are good conductors of heat (such as metal) are poor insulators, and good insulators (such as plastic foam) are poor conductors.

0-7424-2748-X *Hands-On Physics Experiments*

Heat Moves

Kind of cup	Temperature at start	Temperature after 5 minutes	Temperature after 15 minutes

Which cup held heat the best? _____

Which cup lost heat the fastest? _____

0-7424-2748-X *Hands-On Physics Experiments*

Experiment 30 · Join the Circuit

Students construct a simple electrical circuit.
Electrical current must be able to pass through a complete loop to make a circuit.

What You Need:

- 6-volt battery

- Two pieces of insulated wire 1–2 feet long

- 6- or 12-volt light bulb in a porcelain socket

- Screwdriver

- Pocket knife or wire cutter

- Activity sheet on page 69 for each student

What to Do:

1. Use the knife or wire cutter to strip about an inch of insulation from the ends of both wires. Attach one end of a wire to one terminal of the battery and the other end to one of the screws on the light socket. *Does the bulb light up?* With the second wire, connect the other battery terminal and other screw on the socket. *What happens?*

2. Detach one wire from its terminal. *What happens?* Attach the loose wire to the other terminal, so both wires connect to the same terminal. *What happens?*

Let's Talk About It:

The bulb lights up only when it and the battery are linked by a complete circuit. That circuit included both the positive and negative terminals of the battery.

Teacher Tips:

Always use caution when working with batteries and electricity, and be sure your students do, too.

0-7424-2748-X *Hands-On Physics Experiments*

Join the Circuit

Show how to hook up the wires to make a complete circuit.

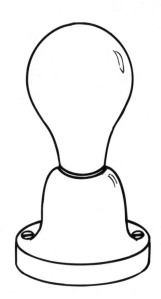

Will the light go on?

Show how to hook up the wires to make an incomplete circuit.

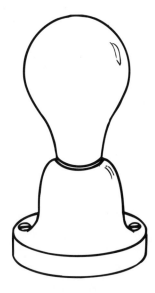

Will the light go on?

0-7424-2748-X *Hands-On Physics Experiments*

Experiment 31 Switch

How does a light switch work?
An electrical switch completes and interrupts a circuit.

What You Need:

- 6-volt battery

- Three pieces of insulated wire 1–2 feet long with bare ends

- Light bulb in a small porcelain socket

- Small block of wood

- Two small nails or metal thumbtacks

- Hammer

- Steel paper clip

- Activity sheet on page 71 for each student

What to Do:

1. Use one wire to connect one battery terminal to a screw on the light socket.

2. Pound the nails or tacks into the wood about an inch apart. Run a wire from one of these nails to the other terminal of the battery. Run another wire from the second nail to the other screw on the socket. *Does the bulb light up?*

3. Fit a paper clip over the first nail so its free end is above the second nail but not touching it. *Does the bulb light up?* Now gently press the paper clip so it touches both nails at the same time. *Does the bulb light up?*

Let's Talk About It:

With the paper clip touching just one nail, the circuit is incomplete and current cannot reach the bulb. When the paper clip touches both nails, it completes the circuit. This requires that current be able to pass through the paper clip. *Where do you use switches in your daily activities?*

Name _____

Date _____

Switch

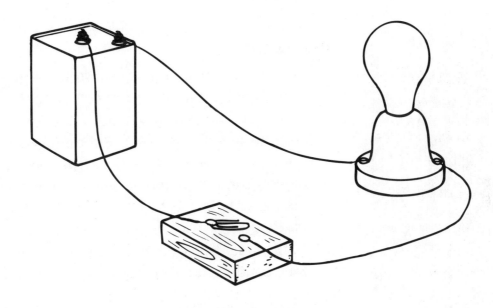

Is this ON or OFF?

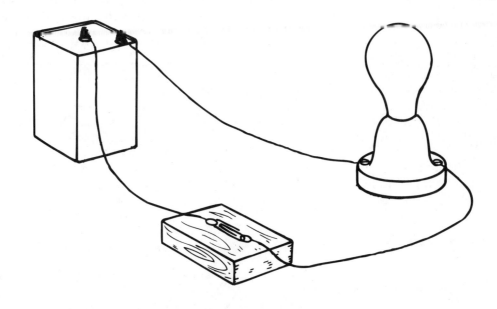

Is this ON or OFF?

Experiment 32 Pass It On

What kinds of materials conduct electricity?
Some materials conduct, or transfer, electrical current.

What You Need:

- Circuit and switch assembly from the previous experiment

- Assortment of objects made of different materials, such as plastic paper clips or comb, wood pencil, metal spoon, a quarter, aluminum foil, steel nail, cloth, paper

- Activity sheet on page 73 for each student

What to Do:

1. Remove the metal paper clip from the switch. *What other items could we use to complete the circuit and make the light turn on?*

2. Test the suggested objects. Put an object in contact with both nails and see if the light bulb goes on. *Which objects conduct electricity? Which ones do not? Do all metals complete the circuit? Does the shape of the object matter?*

3. Help students list the items tested and mark whether they conducted electricity or not.

Let's Talk About It:

Students might be surprised to find that not all metals conduct electricity. Note that you already had evidence that wood does not conduct electricity. Your switch is mounted on wood, yet it does not complete the circuit unless a conducting material connects the two nails.

Pass It On

Objects tested	Material	The light bulb went ON	stayed OFF	Was this a good conductor?

0-7424-2748-X *Hands-On Physics Experiments*

Experiment 33 What's Magnetic?

What kinds of materials are attracted by a magnet?
Magnets attract some materials but not others.

What You Need:

- Magnets

- Assortment of objects made of different materials, such as steel paper clips, nails, pins, leaves, rocks, paper, keys, crayons, soda cans, plastic bottles, and food cans

- Activity sheet on page 75 for each student

What to Do:

1. Have students select objects from your collection. Help them draw or record the names of their objects on their data pages. Have them predict which objects will be attracted to the magnet.

2. Give each student or team a magnet. Have them try to pick up each object with the magnet and mark "yes" or "no" in the appropriate spot on their data sheets.

3. Compare results. Can students reach a general conclusion about what kinds of materials are or are not attracted by magnets?

Let's Talk About It:

Some materials, such as wood and plastic, are never magnetic. Others, such as iron, are always magnetic. Note that not all metals are magnetic. Students can use magnets to sort cans into different bins for recycling of aluminum and steel.

Name _____

Date _____

What's Magnetic?

Objects you tested

Did the magnet pick it up?
Circle your choice.

Yes   No

Yes   No

Yes   No

Yes   No

Use the back of this sheet if you need more room.

0-7424-2748-X *Hands-On Physics Experiments*

Experiment 34 Magnetic Muscle

How strong are magnets?
Magnets vary in strength.

What You Need:

- Small magnets that may all be the same size and shape or may vary

- Steel paper clips

- Activity sheet on page 77 for each student

What to Do:

1. Give each student team a magnet and 25–30 paper clips. If the magnets are different sizes and shapes, have students guess which will be the strongest.

2. Show the students how to make a "chain" of paper clips by picking them up with the magnet one by one and letting them dangle. Teams might have one student hold the magnet, another bring the next paper clip into position, and another to keep count.

3. *How many paper clips will their magnet hold like this? How long is their chain?* Once the limit has been reached, see if another part of the magnet will hold additional paper clips.

4. Compare results. *Which magnet held the longest chain of paper clips? If all the magnets looked the same, did they all hold the same number of paper clips?*

Let's Talk About It:

Each paper clip becomes an extension of the magnet, thus allowing the magnetic force to attract the next paper clip. The force of the magnet declines over distance until finally it is too weak to hold another paper clip.

0-7424-2748-X *Hands-On Physics Experiments*

Magnetic Muscle

Draw your magnet here:

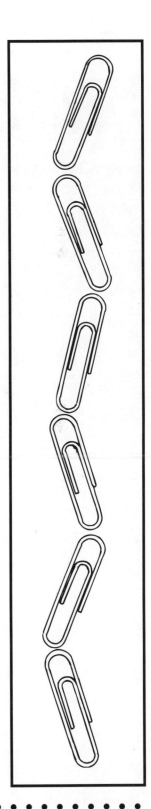

Show how many paper clips
stuck to your magnetic chain.

Published by Instructional Fair. Copyright protected.

0-7424-2748-X *Hands-On Physics Experiments*

Experiment 35 Push and Pull Poles

How do magnets affect each other?
Magnets both attract and repel each other.

What You Need:

- Bar magnets with north and south poles marked

- Rulers

- Activity sheet on page 79 for each student

What to Do:

1. Have each team set two magnets several inches apart on a desk. The ends marked *N* should face each other. Slide one magnet toward the other. *What happens?* Repeat this with the magnets lying next to a ruler. Watch carefully to see how far apart they are when the second magnet starts to move.

2. Turn one magnet so the *N* end of one faces the *S* end of the other. Slide them toward each other. *What happens? How far apart are they when the second magnet starts to move?*

3. Turn the magnets so their long sides face each other, with the two *Ns* at one end and the two *Ss* at the other. Slide them toward each other. *What happens?*
    Turn one magnet around. Slide them toward each other. *What happens?*

Let's Talk About It:

Every magnet has a north pole and a south pole. *Opposite poles (N-S)* attract each other, but *like poles (N-N or S-S)* repel each other. When a magnet is able to move freely, such as when hung from a string, it will line up with Earth's magnetic field. The *N* mark on a magnet means "north-seeking" and the *S* mark means "south-seeking."

0-7424-2748-X Hands-On Physics Experiments

Name _____

Date _____

Push and Pull Poles

What happens?

 attract or repel?

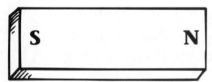 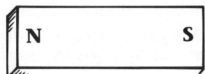 attract or repel?

attract or repel?

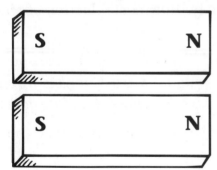 attract or repel?

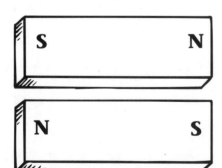 attract or repel?

0-7424-2748-X *Hands-On Physics Experiments*

Discuss real-life uses of narrow beams of light. Examples include automobile headlights, lighthouse beacons, advertising searchlights, and the tiny lights doctors use to examine our eyes and ears.

The greatest source of light on Earth is the sun. Have students measure their own shadows at different times of day. *Is their shadow always behind them? What determines where and how long their shadow will be?*

The sun also provides a link between light and heat energy. Have your students measure the temperature in sunny and shady parts of the classroom or playground at different times of day. *Does the color of an object affect its temperature in the sunlight? How about in the shade?*

As a follow-up to their experiment on heat conduction, help students design an experiment to test whether materials that are good at keeping hot things hot are also good at keeping cold things cold.

After your students have made an electrical circuit to turn on a light bulb, have them experiment with converting electricity into sound. They can build a circuit that powers a buzzer or a doorbell. *Can they see where the switch is in these circuits?*

The terms *conduction* and *insulation* appeared in two contexts in this section—the transfer of heat and the transmission of electricity. *How is conduction similar in these two contexts? Insulation?*

Finally, magnets provide many fun experiments. For example: *Are the south and north poles of a magnet equally strong? Can a magnet attract objects through water? Through solid objects? How can you make a magnet "float" in mid-air?*

0-7424-2748-X *Hands On Physics Experiments*